Why Women Love Jerks:
Realizing the Best Version of
Yourself to Effortlessly Attract
Women (Dating Advice for Men
to Attract Women and Increase
Self-Confidence)

By Patrick King, Dating and Image
Coach at
www.PatrickKingConsulting.com

Why Women Love Jerks: Realizing the Best Version of Yourself to Effortlessly Attract Women (Dating Advice for Men to Attract Women and Increase Self-Confidence)

Introduction

But I don't want to be a jerk!

1. Chase her and she'll run away.

2. If you create a vacuum, she will fill it.

3. Dependence is the ultimate buzzkill… and is so having total control.

4. You are you, and she is only part of that.

5. Anticipation is a super magnet.

6. Act the prize, be the prize.

7. Treat her like a woman, not a daughter.

8. Space is power.

9. You Tarzan, she Jane.

10. Embrace relationship limbo.

11. You do not negotiate with terrorists (relationships).

12. No man taken for granted.

13. The confidence chapter.

14. Be a source of inspiration and challenge.

15. Vulnerability is your goal.

Conclusion

The Jerk Complex cheat sheet.

Introduction

You hear it constantly.

Men will complain that the women they desire simply don't like nice guys like them, and that they are only interested in guys that treat them poorly and don't take care of them. He, of course, has unwittingly placed his "relationship" with that particular woman on a pedestal so high that he can't ever hope to climb it, even though he feels supremely entitled to.

On the other side of the gender fence, women will complain that all of the men she dates treat her like trash and generally seem indifferent to her presence and affections. She, of course, perceives these men as exciting, and doesn't recognize that a nice guy doesn't have to withhold excitement, charm, and personality.

If these sound like two sides of the same coin, it's because they are.

What most people fail to consistently do is to separate the individual personality traits that they are attracted to from the people that they reside in.

Translation – people might think they know what they want, but they often seize the wrong things! Many things look similar or near-identical on the surface level.

Here's a common case in point: a woman believes that she is attracted to independent and masculine men… so she always ends up with men that are emotionally distant and inattentive to her needs because outwardly, they seem similar enough and can be attractive. See the misattribution?

This is what this book is about, uncovers, and seeks to solve.

How can the nice guys of the world (or anyone that just isn't a jerk) harness the flash and raw attractiveness that the jerk possesses in spades? How can we separate the individual jerk personality traits that they display and use them to our advantage in a healthy way?

In other words, how can we remain nice guys but attract women with the best of them?

At the most basic level, it's pattern recognition and correlation analysis. If this is starting to sound scientific, it's because I've broken it down as such. With this in mind, let's revisit the statements from above:

"Women don't like nice guys like me!"

Incoming reality check. Women *love* guys that are nice to them and take care of them. However, they do *not* love the guy who makes them their first, second, and third priority and hangs on her every word and action… or guys who pander to everyone's happiness but their own… or guys that secretly believe that fostering a close friendship with her will one day make her fall for you like a romantic comedy – "It was you all along… you were hiding in plain sight… I love you."

It's pretty easy to see why she would choose a jerk that challenges her and keeps things exciting over that nice guy, despite the negative long-term implications.

"All the guys I date treat me like trash!"

Incoming reality check. Girl, you just played by a guy that just isn't that into you. And let's face it, that probably made you all the more interested and intrigued at the outset. Again, it's easy to see the attractiveness of a guy who loves to march to his own drum and has many priorities in his life besides you… versus a guy who is always there like a clinging, suffocating shadow. Checkmate, jerk once again.

So given that there is a clear disconnect between what people think they want and what they end up getting, the following question is begged: regardless of who you are, how can you embody the traits that people think they want? How can you take advantage of the jerk's traits, remove the jerk part, and embody the parts that women love?

You'll learn exactly how to walk that thin line like an expert in this book.

I'll break down the exact traits that cause women to flock to jerks like moths to a porch light. On the flip side, I'll examine the exact traits that make men get categorized and cast aside as boring, unexciting, and just "nice." Finally, I'll tell you exactly how to ride this phenomenon to success and mastery with women.

Have your female love interests ever told you that they just don't think of you that way, or that they cherish your friendship too much to risk losing it? This book is for you. Do you do fine with the ladies and just want to create the most attractive version of yourself? This book is definitely for you.

Let's shed the stigma from the jerk label and harvest the fruits into… *the Jerk Complex*.

Nice guys *do* finish last… when they don't understand the Jerk Complex.

But I don't want to be a jerk!

This is a point worth repeating. If you've gotten to this point of the book and are still skeptical of my intentions and lessons, you may have missed my main proposition entirely.

The typical perception is that a jerk is careless or indifferent about the women he sees. This might be true of the True Jerk, but I propose that the Jerk Complex is composed of traits that can be construed to look that way, but are actually overwhelmingly positive traits of a well-balanced man.

The word jerk is code for a number of things, and jerk aren't always jerks per se depending on who you are talking to.

For nice guys, "jerk" is code for a guy who doesn't appear to pander to women, even upsetting them at times.

For women, "jerk" is code for a guy who doesn't appear to pander to women, even upsetting them at times.

No, that wasn't a typo. Those descriptions apply to the outward appearance of both the True Jerk and the Jerk Complex. While the True Jerk manifests these because he believes that it will (1) attract women, or (2) he is overcompensating for his own insecurities, the Jerk Complex comes from a place of positivity and self-assurance – independence, conviction in their own beliefs, understanding of their own self-worth and esteem, and indifference to offending the peanut gallery.

He places a high value on his own time, and becomes unavailable and aloof as a result of the dogged pursuit of his passions and hobbies. He also realizes that a relationship, important as it may be, doesn't define him or consume all of his time.

The True Jerk doesn't text or pay much attention because he thinks that doing so will attract women, and he wants to minimize his chances of being rejected as much as possible.

The Jerk Complex will never overtext, and may sometimes be distant because he's so busy living life on his own terms.

It's a collection of personality traits and values that will offend and turn some off by their very nature... but the Jerk Complex is entirely comfortable with it. And of course, that kind of attitude is *guaranteed* to be attractive to women.

So in the context of what we're achieving here, I'm isolating traits that jerks display and turning them into assets for everyone else.

The rest is typical human nature and interaction theory – as will be clearly illustrated through the following principles. After all, studies have shown that inconsistent rewards are addictive – isn't that exactly what jerks do, when broken down in the simplest of terms? You never know when they'll come through, so you are kept on your toes, and the anticipation has built such that when they actually do come through, it's a surprising, joyous occasion.

The Jerk Complex promotes positive internal changes that result in an upgraded social and love life, while staying true to your roots.

1. Chase her and she'll run away.

Flowers, candy, and a cuddly teddy bear.

For some, that sounds like an ideal gift basket to a woman after a few dates. Haven't we been forcefed the notion that women love to be romanced, wined, and dined?

I for one think it would be wiser to use the money you'd spend on all of that on a nice steak for yourself.

This isn't to say that you shouldn't make an effort to pursue and impress a woman that you are interested in. It's simply well-known human nature that when you chase someone, it makes them far less interested in being caught. It makes them bored. It repels them. And if you *overpursue* a woman, it brings the perception that you have nothing better to do, that there are no other women that you're pursuing... and that you aren't a very high-value person in general.

You might even be seen as desperate. After all, doesn't a more charming and overall charismatic person have women and people come to *him*? It's the epitome of the mindset of "If he's chasing me… he must not be worth it!"

We can debate the fairness of such labeling and perceptions all day long, and I'd agree with you that it's judgmental and ridiculous… but still stand my ground on the reality of it.

Pursuing hard also places you in the unenviable position of being labelled a "people pleaser," which is not used here in a positive sense. People subconsciously lose respect for people pleasers, and you will be no exception. Not quite the position you would like to be in with a woman you desire, is it?

The True Jerk never falls prey to this because he truly doesn't care about the woman in question. He will never overpursue because he won't be interested enough to, therefore maintaining his mystique and allure. The True Jerk is confident (perhaps overly so) in himself, and assumes people will come to him. This brash confidence often does draw people to him.

It's human nature to be intrigued by someone that isn't intrigued or captivated by you, and again epitomizes another facet of human nature, "If you tell me I can't, then I want to even more!"

Or even more so, "Everyone wants what they can't have."

But what about the decent man that enjoys a woman's presence and personality, and doesn't want to come off as overpursuing? How can he pursue her in an attractive, optimal way without overdoing it and *over*pursuing? How can the Jerk Complex help us here?

It's a mindset – one that will be emphasized repeatedly in this book. You are a prize of a man, and you shouldn't be compromising your dignity to pursue someone. How can you tell if your dignity is being compromised? Simply do the "tell a friend" test. If you can tell a friend about your pursuit, and you get any negative reactions like eyerolls or groans, you've probably acted without dignity.

This woman, and everything that follows, does not dictate your life or actions. You have a strong sense of self. You are different from the rest of the chumps that will let her walk on their jacket over a puddle, instead of playfully hip-bumping her out of harm's way.

In this mindset, you do not drop everything to pursue a woman… you might not even drop anything. Simply acknowledge your interest in her, and don't overdo it. A large part of why some men feel the need to overpursue is the insecurity that the woman is not truly interested in them, so he needs to do all that he can to ensure that she is. You have to resist this urge because nothing you do inbetween actually spending time with her is going to tip the scales in your favor – it will likely do the opposite and disqualify you mentally.

Women are on the whole more emotionally intelligent than men, and can often intuit what we men are trying to do before we ourselves even know – they will sense your insecurities, and be turned off by them. Overpursuit is a lose-lose situation.

To the men who pay too much attention and feel the need to overpursue, I pose a question: Would you rather win, or would you rather ease your sense of impatience and chivalry? To win, you must leave her wanting more… which will cause her to want it all!

As I'll go over in depth later in this book, emotional uncertainty and a lack of sense of control are amazing aphrodisiacs. (Don't believe me? Ever had sex in a blindfold?) The True Jerk embraces this because he doesn't actually care about a woman, and she thus actually has no control.

The Jerk Complex lives his own life, which mimics how this manifests… which keeps you in control and ultimately a challenge.

And who can resist a challenge?

2. If you create a vacuum, she will fill it.

The mind has a funny way of playing tricks on us. If something is less attainable, such as a jerk who doesn't seem to care, they are automatically alluring and attractive for that very reason.

From the previous chapter, we learned that things that pursue us are automatically repulsive and imply a lower value. This applies to all walks of life – don't we have tenfold desire for things we are told we can't have?

Now here's a powerful trick that True Jerks have known all along and that everyone else should be utilizing: if you can subtly create a vacuum (a void where your presence and communications used to be), that makes a woman make more of an effort to be with you. It essentially makes her chase you, and eventually she will begin to believe her actions… and believe that you are worth the chase.

The True Jerk of course creates the vacuum by not actually caring about people, but everyone else can take advantage by simply analyzing human interaction.

And it has huge implications.

If you create a vacuum and don't chase, you create the perception that you are otherwise busy, and don't or can't prioritize her. It's a fine line, but this perception is typically positive for you. It's what high-value people do.

When you create a vacuum, it is inevitable that she will seek to eliminate it by moving closer to you. She may wonder what you're doing with your time, think you're more attractive, or just plain be bored. Whatever the reason, there's going to be something niggling in her mind about you. Subsequently, when you stay still and she moves towards you, that's essentially her pursuing you. She probably won't even realize it, as the mind does the rest. Witness the inner monologue:

First: "Hey, I wonder what Joe's been up to lately?

Then: "Say... I haven't seen Joe lately..."

More: "Is he ignoring me for another girl...?"

Finally: "Why didn't I ever date Joe...?"

The mind has a tendency to wander like a tumbleweed, and when you create a vacuum, the tumbleweed will inevitably drift to you and believe that there is a reason for that drift.

For example, what do men think of when we're pursuing a woman? We are chasing because we think we know what we want, and often times gameplanning our next move. Regardless of how much we like her, the woman occupies a sizeable piece of our mental bandwidth for hours a week. And so will you occupy *her* mind and consciousness during a vacuum. She might even think that she caused the vacuum or is at fault for it, and seek to win you back and make amends.

Creating a vacuum will also cause people to automatically respect you and defer to you more because they won't feel that they have the upper hand on you – which gives you the upper hand. When someone isn't present, we tend to forget the power imbalance that there might have previously been and are just grateful for their returning presence.

So how do you create the all-important vacuum with a woman? How does the Jerk Complex effectively use a vacuum to his advantage?

It's simple. Live your glorious life, and don't be available at her beck and call. In fact, sometimes make it a point to be scarce and absent. Focus on your other priorities, and *demote her*. Don't accommodate her, or give in to your urges to see her or rekindle your friendship.

Chances are that if you're in love with a friend, the friendship itself isn't really based on anything real.

Don't reply immediately to her – because you're a busy man! I would even go so far as to ignore and distance yourself from the object of your affection for a period of weeks to create the vacuum. You can then judge her interest level by whether she fills it at all. Women are masters of subtly – sometimes they use so much that their intended targets don't even realize it! But women can also chase very directly simply because they can get away with it.

In those direct instances, don't cave immediately, even if you want to. As I will cover later, anticipation and the chase is one of the biggest aphrodisiacs known to man other than Marvin Gaye.

Ultimately, people chase prizes. By letting her close the distance and fill the vacuum, you have sneakily taken the place of the prize and object of her affection and goals – and she will believe that.

3. Dependence is the ultimate buzzkill... and is so having total control.

Let's picture a bloodsucking parasitic leech for a moment. A leech is completely dependent on you for sustenance, activity, and life. It will be drastically hurt if separated from you, and generally cannot survive without you. We do not like leeches... whether they are actual leeches or the human equivalent.

When something is overly dependent on us, every human has the immediate reaction of regret, wanting to withdraw, and general disgust. The first instinct is to create distance, not in a purposeful vacuum sort of way, and to seize their independence again.

When someone is dependent on you, your independence is inextricably linked to theirs, and they have just made you lose yours. It hamstrings your sense of independence and imposes a burden of guilt and obligation that you haven't chosen for yourself.

Being entirely dependent and clingy on a woman like a leech will cause her to quickly lose respect for you and take you for granted. Who notices or cares about the shadow that is omnipresent? This book is about creating the most attractive version of yourself, and there is nothing attractive about a shadow that needs you to live.

This loss of respect and taking you for granted will inevitably set the tone for a relationship that will be unbalanced in every way… and you will be at the short end of the stick every time. Clinginess and dependence gives the woman the pants to the relationship, the keys to the house, and ownership of the danglers inside your pants.

Everyone outside of your relationship will also take notice, and that's not a kind impression for people to have about you. About .0001% of the female population wants this kind of relationship dynamic with their significant other. How many times have you heard that a woman likes someone to take charge, be dominant and masculine?

That is perhaps the encompassing issue with clinginess and dependence – it denotes a lack of masculinity and strength that women innately and explicitly seek. In other words, they don't want control of a relationship, and certainly not the total control that a dependent man gives them. At worst, it's an incredible turnoff.

Guess what the True Jerk never does? That's right, become dependent on others. This might be because he is too selfish or self-absorbed, but the True Jerk generally does not open himself up to the vulnerability of being dependent on someone else because he is scared of what may follow.

Alternatively, the Jerk Complex dictates that your first priority is yourself and your time (in case realizing that women don't like to be smothered isn't enough). When you value yourself and display your independence, women will follow suit. Think about the reason we all consider delaying replying to emails and texts – it's because we want to maintain an air of busyness and independence. We innately recognize the value of this.

When you can create a lifestyle for yourself that truly is self-centered to an extent (and this term isn't used in a negative sense here!) and independent, you will also develop the strength and masculinity that women crave and seek out.

A huge aspect of chemistry is the concept of equality and meeting your match. When you have your strengths and she has hers, the power balance is nearly equal and matches have been met – this leads to a great mutual respect. And with such a good balance, there is always an amount of uncertainty because you never quite feel like you have the upper hand, so there is always sexual tension, effort, and a subtle chase and dance.

When the balance is tipped either way with someone being clingy and dependent, someone will become the reacher in the relationship, and someone will become the settler. Respect will wane. There will be a clear upper hand. This leads to a negative cycle of spurts of effort, and periods of complacency that plague all unhealthy relationships.

And guess where that ultimately ends?

4. You are you, and she is only part of that.

Pussy-whipped.

It's a jarring term, and one that guys tend to treat like the plague. It means that you as a man have subordinated yourself to a woman, regardless of whether you are benefitting from that relationship or not. You cater to her needs more than your own, and put her on a pedestal so high that you can't ever hope to climb it.

What is central to being unattractively pussy-whipped is the fact that you have lost your individuality, which has been demoted to a secondary priority. Obviously, this is insane, but it's not like most pussy-whipped men consciously make the choice to do this. It's a series of small decisions and forks in the road that lead one to the kingdom of the pussy-whipped – allow me to map the path.

First: "Sure, I'll come pick you up instead of grabbing a beer with my buddies!"

Next: "Don't worry about it, I was in the neighborhood anyway."

More: "Hey, I'm free anytime Monday-Friday, just let me know what works for you!"

Finally: "No, I totally understand, it was super last minute that your friend came into town so you cancelled on me!"

If any of those statements look remotely familiar…

This chapter is about maintaining your independence and individuality outside of your significant other or woman that you are pursuing.

Let's take a look at our trusty True Jerk.

Maybe he's selfish, or maybe he just doesn't care that much about the women he's involved with. Maybe he is dating few at once. Whatever the case, he keeps a healthy (or unhealthy!) separation from the woman and keeps his own priorities as number one. He doesn't accommodate woman, and he isn't defined by his relationships with women.

He will hang out with friends almost the same amount as when he is single as when he is with someone. What the True Jerk manifests as disinterest, the Jerk Complex manifests as a sense of strength and independence. You are not dependent on her, do not need her, and will be fine without her. Never let someone else define your world.

Just because she has injected passion into your life doesn't mean that she is the only thing you can be passionate about!

One of the biggest aspects of losing your individuality is that men will slowly but surely stop standing up to or asserting themselves with women. They become okay with anything the woman decides and are resigned to the decidedly dictatorial process they now reside under. It's a process that leads to being walked all over. As you can see from the above thought bubbles, sometimes it's so subtle that you don't even realize that it happens.

But to expand on the Jerk Complex's mindset, your decisions shouldn't be based on whether they retain the woman. You have your own principles that you should stay true to. If you constantly compromise your principles and identity for someone else, people will naturally begin to lose respect for you. If you back up and view yourself from someone else's perspective, you may lose respect for yourself as well.

How many times have you heard anyone, woman or man, remark that they want someone that has their own passions and pursuits? If we trim away all the usual sunshine and rainbows attached to that statement, it really means at the root that they don't want to be the center of someone's universe. They don't want to be responsible for someone's happiness, sadness, highs, and lows.

It's a lot of pressure, and frankly, it gets old. What are they getting out of that relationship at that point?

People like to be prioritized, but when they are the number one priority at every waking moment, it becomes scary even for the most committed. For every dependent act you make, you inadvertently chain the other person to the label of "Jim AND Karen" which is cause for potential resentment and avoidance.

Women want someone that can stand toe to toe with them, because dating and relationships are about finding partners and companions, not pussy-whipped sycophants. Sometimes this means that arguments will end relationships or become more serious than they would have otherwise. This is not an entirely negative thing, because again... you do not need her, and you are your own strong individual.

When you are engaged in something, you become engaging – and being engaged in the other person doesn't count!

5. Anticipation is a super magnet.

I'm a big hobbyist, and believe strongly in pursuing as many hobbies and skills as possible.

My latest endeavor is woodcarving, and it's truly been one of the biggest challenges of my life. I've always been good with my hands and have even done some forms of woodworking and construction in the past, but there is something about manipulating the knives I just can't quite grasp. And you know what? That makes me want to excel at it that much more, and I know that the ensuing victory will be that much more satisfying and triumphant.

What does this have to do with jerks, the Jerk Complex, and becoming attractive to women?

The longer you have to wait for something you want, like mastering woodcarving, the more you want it. This phenomenon of human desires transfers exactly to dating, courting, and relationships.

The longer a woman has to wait for someone she is interested in, the more she is going to want and appreciate him when she gets him. And if she doesn't get him, she will probably want him (you) even more!

Of course, this is "the chase" that we all know and love/hate. There's a reason that many people look back on the chase phase as the best part of their relationships, and it certainly evokes powerful emotions.

In the context of this book, I'm defining the chase in the following manner: the gentle and delicate interplay between how much interest and reciprocation is allowed to be shown in a courtship. Let's unpack that.

The gentle and delicate interplay… it must be so, because an unspoken rule of the game is that you are not playing the game. Bear with me. The aim is to make your lower level of interest and reciprocation appear natural, because if the other party figures out that you are indulging in the chase, it is automatically seen as *higher* interest and reciprocation.

Shake your head all you want, but embrace it.

How much interest and reciprocation is allowed to be shown… as I've discussed before, there is a delicate power balance of meeting your match, and skewing too much one way or the other will upset that balance and project the perception that you have lower value and aren't in demand.

Playing the chase correctly will create the anticipation of desiring something you can't have at the moment, but just close enough and plausible enough to keep you motivated and hungry for it (her). Studies have shown that inconsistent rewards are scientifically proven to motivate us more and evoke greater feelings of reward and satisfaction – apply this to your interactions with women.

The True Jerk keeps anticipation high by acting aloof and generally plays the chase excellently because he doesn't forecast much interest, if any. The Jerk Complex allows us to emulate those emotions by simply realizing that uncertainty is a powerful precursor to anticipation, which is a powerful driving force in human relationships.

As with before, keep your plans and activities for yourself. Keep your own priorities. Don't always pick up her calls or answer her texts in a timely manner. If she doesn't contact you at the proposed time, move on and make other plans.

Employ push and pull techniques where you show her attention in bursts when you're free, and zero attention when you're busy with other matters. There's no manipulation here – you're just doing what you can according to your busy social schedule.

If you stay in a perpetual chase phase by keeping anticipation high (and availability low) with any woman you think that there is potential with, you build tension, attraction, and handily avoid the friendzone.

6. Act the prize, be the prize.

One of the failings of the many men's dating mindsets is rooted in the inequalities of the dating economy.

Because women are seemingly in such short supply and men generally have a more difficult time engaging with women, many men will take the position of accepting whatever scraps a woman will give them. Of course, this is a system where men also enable women to act this way because men accept and even encourage it, preferring it over nothing.

They are the modern-day versions of Oliver Twist humbly begging for more soup.

These men, which you will no longer be a part of, simply don't act the prize, so women don't view them as one. My message in this chapter is simple – if you act the prize, women will begin to treat you and view you like one.

The True Jerk acts the prize because he may genuinely think he is better than others, and thus imposes that belief on others. He may not cause others to view him as such, but a little arrogance and overconfidence is decidedly more attractive than acting like you're grateful that a woman gave you some attention.

How exactly does a prize act within the humble and unassuming Jerk Complex?

It's not about acting like you're all that and a bag of chips.

A prize just acts like his time is precious, and that people should be grateful for his presence. A prize isn't at anyone's beck and call, and certainly doesn't accept only scraps of attention that someone decides to give them. A prize takes pride in his own interests and zealously values his time.

As said before, if you believe yourself a prize (or at least fake it), then others will follow your lead. The prize has more dignity and pride in himself than ancillary attention from a woman can conquer.

A prize has confidence in himself and his capabilities, and doesn't let himself be disrespected or taken for granted. Confidence is a topic for an entire book by itself (and an entire chapter later), but is an amazing aphrodisiac in itself.

The important question herein is really whether others view you as a prize, and how you must change that perception of your priority.

Here are some litmus questions for if you are viewed as a prize or priority. How far ahead of time are plans made with you? Does she inquire about your schedule? Does she try to reschedule with you if she cancels or postpones? Does she cancel on other people to see you?

Case in point - booty calls are one of the greatest inventions since vacation sex and putting on socks fresh out of the dryer. However, booty calls are sometimes motivated by emotions that aren't the most positive, despite the benefits you might be getting. Don't mistake her contacting you as spontaneity and longing.

If you're getting a call at 2:00 AM, you can feel free to cheer and start cleaning your room, but I propose that you should think about exactly why the call came so late. Namely, that you are the backup for the night, and are better company than no one at all – not quite a prize, is it?

So if you really value cultivating your image as a prize, resist answering that call, no matter how much you want to hitch the train to bonecity. You will drastically change the perception of power in that relationship, and make yourself a challenge that she must conquer.

A prize doesn't accept being treated like a backup. If someone doesn't hold you in the regard of a prize, why do you want to be with someone like that... or in a relationship that is already so unbalanced and skewed towards satisfying only her?

A prize doesn't apologize to women purely out of instinct and to avoid conflict; he requires a clear reason because a prize knows his worth and doesn't pander to others. If she asks how your schedule is the next day, give only a couple of specific openings, because a prize is constantly keeps himself busy and fills his schedule quickly. A prize doesn't accept poor treatment from women and will show displeasure accordingly.

This process begins within. When you clearly treat yourself like a priority, others will take notice and follow.

7. Treat her like a woman, not a daughter.

Whether you're a fan of it or not, chivalry is still very much alive and kicking. All women are romantics at heart, and their fairytale romances almost always begin and end with a prince that sweeps them off their feet. They want and desire to be taken care of, and men often feel the reciprocal need to be the protector and caretaker.

Chivalry is in a sense, directly tied to our modern day conception of romance.

But chivalry is taking care of your woman in the primal way that a man does for his mate... and not in the way that a father takes care of his daughter. Your interactions must straddle the sometimes thin line between your chivalrous instincts and smothering father territory.

Fathering has the distinct effect of making someone feel smothered and that they are being tracked by someone for their own purposes – not that they are being taken care of and treated like a princess.

For those of you that did not have overbearing fathers growing up, here's what fathers do: ask you where they were, ask you to check in with them, account for time away from them, be overly clingy and focused on you, place their own expectations on you, be preachy about what you're doing and who you're seeing, dote too much, and assume that will be spent together.

Now that we're all working within the same context – how does someone like that make you feel?

Probably annoyed, smothered, mothered, and ultimately wanting to break free and get away? "Whew, thank God I got away from him for the night! He's too much!" Yup, you're creating the same effect in a woman when you treat them like a daughter and not like a mate.

Some women ultimately come to the conclusion that they want to marry someone very similar to their father – but absolutely not in this aspect. They spent (around) eighteen years living under the same roof with them and taking orders from them already, they don't want any more!

You will create the same instinct that a woman will feel if you overly dote and become dependent and clingy on her. She'll feel cornered and instantly look for an escape route... and by creating that distance, it instantly turns you into the pursuer. We've gone over why this is a losing proposition for you. She might even lash out against you as a daughter would to her father setting her curfew.

Finally, women don't often have romantic chemistry with their fathers or anyone that they feel is nagging and watching them like a hawk.

Even if she likes you and doesn't mind the excessive amount of attention and oversight, you create a negative association with each of your interactions – she will feel obligated to spend time with you, and may even do so out of guilt. You're putting your expectations on someone else, and anytime that happens, they will feel burdened to have to live up to them.

Is it positive to have someone spend time with you out of a feeling of duty or guilt? Of course not! Your time spent together and dates should be highly anticipated and looked forward to.

So how does the Jerk Complex treat his mate, where the True Jerk just doesn't care? He protects her, but he doesn't dote on her safety. He takes care of her, but doesn't nag that everything is in order. He protects her but doesn't make her carry her rape whistle. He takes advantage of the romantic side and charming side of chivalry and doesn't stay mired in treating her like a princess. The Jerk Complex can take care of himself, and assumes that his woman can as well.

He is her prince charming and takes her out on dates, but he doesn't tell her about the history of the restaurant's pizza and prevent her from eating pepperoni.

Your focus should be on romantic gestures that a mate uses for seduction, and not overbearing fatherly gestures that will drive her to rebel against you. Contact her to demonstrate that you miss her, but not to make sure that she's okay, had her vitamins, and hear about every detail.

8. Space is power.

There's a saying that goes "If you love someone, set them free… and if they return to you, then it was meant to be."

Of course, it's bullshit. If you want that to happen, buy a boomerang.

If you give someone the space they want, they'll almost never look back. The saying mostly gives people a hopeful silver lining in the context of a breakup. But ending this chapter right there wouldn't be useful, would it?

Space, when given like a release from jail, is not going to help you. But when you cleverly give *yourself* space, that void will only serve to draw women to you.

My point is probably worth a repeat.

When you give women too much space and time to themselves, it's not a guarantee that they'll come back to you… they may just run from you or get bored – further, this takes matters out of your hands, which is never the goal.

However, when you give *yourself* the same space and freedom, to talk to other women for example, they will take note immediately and come running back.

How does the Jerk Complex expertly give himself the same space that a woman might crave? It's pretty easy if you think about it for a second. What kind of freedom would women not want to see you with, and make them feel like they don't have the upper hand anymore?

First of all, don't define your relationship at the first hint of ambiguity – it's that ambiguity that will drive her back to you and keep you intriguing. Once you talk about your relationship and become exclusive, you are indicating to her that you are committing to her, and eliminating even the possibility of space.

This is positive in a general sense, but for a Jerk Complex's pursuit and endeavour in becoming attractive to a woman the space in uncertainty is important. Space retains chase and mystery. If she wanted The Talk, she would have scheduled it herself. Make her secretly beg for it and force your hand.

Chances are that if you project this air of avoiding the relationship and exclusivity talk, even if that's what you want, she will try to change your mind. Sometimes it's not even personal at that point, but a challenge to her and her pride. She will want to close the space, and won't be happy seeing you with your own.

There are similar effects if you tell her you are unsure about wanting to be with her exclusively, or unsure about wanting to do long-distance... insure about wanting to date because you are coworkers... it's just going to make her want to convince you otherwise.

Second, as you have given her space in all aspects of her life... you also have space and freedom in all aspects of your life. This means in terms of talking to other women, and dating them. This is really what women mean by their desire of space, so it's only fair play that you experience the same space. What follows will be eye-opening (if they are aware of the subtle hints and call-outs to your new space and lifestyle that you make public).

They'll suddenly begin checking in more with you. Randomly texting you and saying hello. Asking you to hang out more. Making time for you in their schedule. Planning a week or two ahead for you.

It's the same effect and reason that you shouldn't openly compete with other males for her – it's devaluing, and shows that you can't deal with your own space.

They think you've given the space that they desire, but once they see how desirable you also are and happy you can be without her, it will drastically change her opinion on space. Such is the power of choice that you've introduced – choice is exciting, and we largely believe that all of our own choices are made for reasons we know.

So when you give her space and the freedom to select you or someone else, and they select you, they will believe that it is a genuine choice of chemistry and attraction. This is partially true – the only asterisk is that the chemistry and attraction is due to the space that you've given them that they want to fill. You have just turned into the pursued, as she wants to close the space.

Third, people are typically intrigued by those that aren't immediately available to them. Simple human nature that has been covered, and will be covered again, in this book. Just as I was so driven and satisfied by attempting to master woodcarving, so will the women be in trying to master you. Once you introduce space, you become woodcarving to them – presently unattainable, but seemingly worth the effort and wait.

Finally, you must embrace the emotional and mental space from her. Do not be emotionally dependent on her, and maintain your own interests and hobbies. This is another very real void that she will begin to feel almost immediately – it will remind her of how positive and fun of an influence on her life that you have, and not allow her to use you purely as an emotional crutch, AKA the friendzone.

If they see you giving other women the duties and privileges of someone that you want to date, they will want them back immediately. Subsequently, she will feel lucky to be with you: the independent man who has given her space, but has really just taken his own.

9. You Tarzan, she Jane.

Even if you're dating a woman who is a high-powered CEO, chances are that she doesn't want to be in control of your relationship. In fact, it's a good bet that she wants the exact opposite.

She wants a manly Tarzan that allows her to take a backseat and be Jane. There are exceptions to the rule, but many (if not most) women are completely fine satisfying the gender role of wanting to be taken care of.

The True Jerk does this because he has little regard for a woman's feelings, and takes control of the interaction because he is focused only on himself. He doesn't stop to consider other people's preferences or opinions, and leads without ever looking back.

Again, we see a theme of indifference being mistaken as confidence.

The Jerk Complex on the other hand simply recognizes that her instinct to be feminine is very real and palpable, and can only be satisfied when you assume the masculine and dominating role. Make her feel like she can be Betty Homemaker or Hilda Housewife, and that's a role she will embrace to the fullest. Act towards that goal and the rest will follow.

Giving her those feelings is extremely powerful because they appeal to a woman's primal feelings. You essentially because the man that she wants. Instill a sense of safety in her. Open jars and kill bugs for her. Hold her umbrella or give her your coat. Park the car for her. Set a date by telling her only the time, location, and outfit to wear.

It's hard to do that if she's making all the decisions and directing your interactions. So be the dominant man that she wants to sweep her off her feet. If you act that way, you'll project the confidence and masculinity and she desires. And just as importantly, the dominant man doesn't stay mired in insecurity.

On the surface level, some might call it chivalry, but that's a different mindset completely. Here, you are taking control of the interaction simply because you are the type of man to do so, not out of respect or deference to her, or to pamper her and "treat her like a lady."

This means that indecision is one of the most unattractive traits possible. The following type of exchange is strictly forbidden:

"What do you want to do/eat/see next?"

"I don't know, what do you want to do? I don't care."

So it's up to you to take control and plan the entire date with segmentation and backup options. You will lead the date through your segments. You will take care of the directions and not ask her to look up the address. You will provide a blanket, umbrella, or gloves just in case she needs them. You will deal with the bill (not necessarily paying) and address any issues that arise with the date itself. You will deal with the transportation. You will lead her through crowds. You will introduce her to the chef of the restaurant. I think you get it.

If you lead, she will take notice and follow suit. Most importantly, she'll respect you and your capabilities, which can write a one-way ticket away from the friend zone.

Practice tip: plan the next outing for you and your friends. Take care of all the planning details, the hiccups, dealing with waiters, splitting the check, renting the home, and controlling the guest list. This will let you know exactly what's needed for such an event (or date), and will give you experience and confidence in your abilities to take control. It will also make you more comfortable with potential confrontation when you have to fix or remedy a situation on a date.

However, note that there is a canyon of distinction between taking charge of the interaction and being one of the guys that will carry her purse for her. Take care of her, but don't cater to her. I like to utilize what I call the *groan test* here. If you can tell your male friends about something you did for her and their reaction is *groaning*, then you are probably catering to her too much.

10. Embrace relationship limbo.

There's always that stage when you're dating someone where you don't know what to call each other. Your friend, girlfriend... whether or not to label them, invent a label, or how to introduce them to your friends. You haven't talked about the terms of the relationship yet, but it seems like there is mutual interest to move forward in some fashion.

Maybe you have a potential date with someone else lined up, but you don't know if that's kosher at this point – after all, if you feel guilty, isn't there something to be guilty about?

And so on.

I urge you to resist throwing your hands up and clearing the air with a "So... what are we?" talk for this simple reason:

Uncertainty is incredibly, incredibly arousing.

Blindfolds during sex. Anticipation before a rollercoaster. This is relationship limbo, and you get the picture. Tension remains high, because every word or date could be the last.

Talking about the relationship has a few negative effects on your approach and mindset with someone, with only one real benefit – settling the uncertainty. In reality, this only tends to benefit the woman in the pre-relationship, because women hate uncertainty and tend to want to cement relationships before they might even be ready.

This may dip into sexist territory, but it is simple human female biology and mindset at work. The primitive woman always sought to find a primitive man that would provide for her and take care of her children – the relationship. Studies have even shown that women desire affirmation in many other forms, and without it, they will seek it out from you in more subtle ways. This is positive for you.

When she seeks subtle affirmation from you, she'll try harder to capture your attention and fish for your time. As we've seen with other subtle points in this book, this leads to her being the pursuer, and eventually actions will transform her mentality of viewing you as the desired prey. Her effort will skyrocket, and you will only stand to benefit.

Remaining in relationship limbo also means that she won't feel like she has a 100% hold on you. This precedes a very subtle shift in the power balance of a relationship, and can instantly shift the pants back to you if they had ever left.

As always, the True Jerk is an expert at this and things that generally make him appear aloof, mysterious, and attractive. He simply doesn't care enough about the woman to entertain thoughts of a relationship, and doesn't bother to confirm that with her. Moreover, he may have commitment issues and only uses women for sex instead of treating them with the respect they deserve. Finally, he may never have been in a real relationship before, period.

So how does the Jerk Complex stand to profit here? This chapter might embody the simplest principle in the book. Do not bring up the future of the relationship. You can talk about it in future terms, but only the immediate future such as next week. Don't talk about what you're going to do together next year. Don't succumb to her pressure. Don't end up relinquishing your edge and your rightful role as the prey and pursued.

When you exit relationship limbo, you place expectations on both you and her that can be difficult to live up to. This means that you are automatically back into the role of the pursuer, because she will expect you to fulfill those expectations. It's not a stretch to posit that women often have higher expectations of men in terms of time and attention, so guess what – you're now expected to provide all of that, to *chase*. And this time, you are obligated to do so.

Of course, this isn't to say that committed relationships are a negative thing. The distinction that I am making is that relationship limbo can be used to jumpstart a healthy relationship with high levels of attraction and seduction.

Too many men are eager to jump into relationships when they aren't ready, or when doing so would be a turnoff to the woman. So when you finally have that relationship-defining talk with her... be aware that you're not only locking yourself down.

11. You do not negotiate with terrorists (relationships).

You grew up in Pittsburgh. You had tons of hobbies as a kid, and played every sport known to man. You have a terrible singing voice, but you like to karaoke anyway. These days, you play in an indoor soccer league every Tuesday, work out twice a week otherwise, and would like to train for a triathlon soon. You've got a few college friends in the area and regularly hit up happy hours after work to socialize and unwind. One time you got into a bike accident where you chipped your front teeth and you looked like a hick for a couple of weeks.

And then it all stops.

We've all seen that scenario before, haven't we? You (or a friend) is as active and outgoing as can be, living life to the fullest, and it all suddenly disappears when they get into a relationship. Their sole focus is on spending time with their paramour, and any other priority gets dropped like a hot potato.

Their relationship has taken them hostage, and they have negotiated everything in their life for the relationship's sake.

The Jerk Complex abides by a no negotiation policy. You've worked hard to cultivate an image for yourself, and really a complete identity independent of anyone else's influence or grasp. You know what you like, and what do you like to do. So keep doing them!

When you begin a relationship, it can be difficult to see past the rose-colored lenses of the honeymoon period. Infatuation almost dictates that you spend an inordinate amount of time together, and generally ignore all other priorities. But this is not sustainable.

If we follow that trend, you two will eventually become each other's world. You will become extremely interdependent, and ultimately lose your identity. You won't be known as Jim anymore – you'll be JimAndCathy.

The Jerk Complex does not negotiate his free time, his hobbies, his values, his ambitions, his friends, or his identity for the sake of the relationship.

Consider this a long-winded way of saying that you cannot let a woman change who you are.

Now consider how attractive the True Jerk is because he simply doesn't care about the woman very much. He is both physically and emotionally unavailable. Whatever the case, he remains himself, and doesn't kowtow to a woman's schedule or demand. He will never negotiate.

Ultimately, a woman likes a man who has a strong sense of self. How many times have you heard a woman say that she wants a guy with passions? This is the usable translation of that statement – please know who you are and stick to that!

Here's a partial list of how the Jerk Complex can stay true to himself:

1. Don't cancel your plans for her.
2. Form internal guidelines on how many times you see her a week.
3. No means no – you're a busy guy and shouldn't always prioritize her over your hobbies and other friends.
4. Remember that you have other friends and attempt to spend time with them accordingly.
5. No flaking (by her) is allowed – your time is precious!
6. Don't make decisions based on "I miss her" or "I just want to see her."

Having a strong sense of self with your own priorities is inherently attractive – as has been implied many times in this book. It inherently raises your value when you reduce the priority of someone else. When you're engaged, you become amazingly engaging.

If you lose that about yourself, you are essentially writing a one-way ticket to the friendzone. You literally will have nothing to add to the relationship other than a warm body and your presence – what about you will a woman admire or even respect?

Moreover, if you were to lose yourself, what will happen if and when you breakup or separate? You are left with a shell of yourself, and a blinding realization that you have truly let yourself go in many ways. Few, if any friends. It's a bleak epiphany that many men reach too late.

Control over yourself – the discipline and drive to continue to pursue your interests and passions can sometimes be difficult, especially when you have to choose between them and your honey's sweet and tender embrace. But maintaining control here, and stopping the relationship terrorists, is integral to maintaining control in the relationship.

Many things are out of our hands, but if you make the sometimes difficult choice to be interesting, and not interested... then that is the key to skyrocketing attraction as a Jerk Complex would.

The obvious other hand is that there needs to be a keen balance struck between your own time, and time spent together for a healthy relationship. She does need to be a priority. But far too many men skew the other way, and are confused why their women grow bored and restless.

Look at it this way: you have a vibrant life on your own, and she is but a wonderful addition to it, though not essential.

Prioritize yourself above all else.

12. No man taken for granted.

I have a few friends that are lawyers, and I believe they'll especially appreciate the points I'm about to make about being taken for granted.

Lawyers have a tough job.

Their very profession is in making sure that the Ts are crossed and that the Is are dotted – exact perfection is expected every single time. If things go well, the lawyer is never congratulated, because that means things have just gone as planned... but if things go wrong with the paperwork, you better believe that they will have hell to pay.

They basically have one of the most thankless jobs in the world because they are taken for granted by their clients, who only seem to have something to say when something goes wrong.

Where am I going with this? Lawyers are taken for granted by their clients because they are simply expected to produce results regardless of the situation or deadline... but unfortunately, that's just in their job description.

Sadly, many men are similarly taken for granted by the women they are dating because they continue to deliver regardless of the situation as if they were obligated to.

Translation: if you are a presence in a woman's life regardless of how busy you yourself are, you are probably being taken for granted.

On the surface, this sounds a bit manipulative and nefarious, but I assure you that there are strong grounds for this simple act. When you are there with a woman constantly, you are like her shadow. She will simply always assume that you will be there because... you HAVE always been there. Your actions have proven her to be right, so why should she assume any different or place any value on your presence if it is constant?

The best thing you can say about a person who is always present and taken for granted is that they are dependable... not entirely flattering, and certainly not a compelling reason to be with someone. Dependable also tends to impart a lack of excitement, allure, mystery, spontaneity, attraction... and a slew of other adjectives that make the Jerk Complex all the more important.

The True Jerk, again, is a master of all things that simulate distance and indifferent to a woman. He is never taken for granted because he is not there very much. Since he is not reliable to be there, his presence is sometimes a surprise an always welcome as found money.

As always, the Jerk Complex finds a stance in the thin gray area between being a True Jerk and a taken for granted shadow. This is a matter of not acting in a way that lets her take you for granted, and to make her respect and cherish your time. All of her actions should prompt reactions from you, as opposed to completely catering to her, which... you got it, leads to being taken for granted.

First, predictable routines and events are the backbone of being taken for granted. Stop that. Try to inject spontaneity and unpredictability into your relationship and life, even if you have to plan it. I should make it clear that your spontaneity should *not* include randomly surprising her with chocolates and roses. That's just going to further her taking you for granted, because instead of being a constant presence in her life, you are now a constant presence + random gifts, which only raises her expectations for you.

Second, you are not clay. Don't be so malleable in your priorities to make her the first and only priority on your mind. Don't cancel on other people to see her. Don't make decisions based on wanting to see her, or just wanting to hang out with her. You should have other priorities and interests in your life, so indulge them!

Making personal concessions and sacrifices to spend time with her will signal that she can have her cake and eat it too... which she will expect from that point on. It's not healthy, sustainable, or attractive in the slightest. Staying busy on your own terms breeds respect and desire.

Third, don't be afraid to ruffle her feathers. Being taken for granted probably means that you are one of the most agreeable people in the world, despite the opinions you hold. You are entitled to your opinions, and entitled to get mad when someone doesn't respect them. When someone takes you for granted, they are likely steamrolling over you and not even realizing that you are the one that is compromising. When you stand up for yourself and put your foot down, it can sometimes jolt people back to appreciative reality – or at least prove a point.

Finally, observe what happens when you take away the woman's girlfriend duties and give them to someone else – in essence, taking *her* for granted so much so that you don't expect anything from her. Allow someone else, male or female, to do her duties and praise them for it. She will want the duties back immediately, and for the first time feel what being taken for granted is like.

Everyone wants to feel desirable to their significant other, and part of that is direct appreciation for what they do for us.

13. The confidence chapter.

In a prior chapter, I begged you to act the prize and therefore become the prize. Displaying confidence and manifesting it is one of the keys to the true Jerk Complex and cementing attraction with anyone.

This is a process that isn't the easiest for some because it can require faking it, some bravado, and acting entirely out of character at times.

This is unfortunate, as it hints strongly at a deeper issue of self-confidence and self-worth. How can you act the prize when inside you feel nothing remotely like it? The logical benefits aside, our own limiting beliefs can sometimes be the bane of our very existence. And of course, if we are limited by our own beliefs and don't have true confidence in ourselves, how can we expect others to hold us in high regard?

There are no jerks of either type without confidence – though it should be noted that the True Jerk works with insecure confidence, while the Jerk Complex works with true confidence.

This is the pep talk chapter. The build-you-up chapter. The chapter where I convince you that you are indeed a prize, and that your confidence and actions should reflect it. Let's begin with some of my favorite quotes on confidence.

Sex appeal is fifty percent of what you've got and fifty percent what people think you've got. – Sophia Loren

To succeed in life, you need two things: ignorance and confidence. – Mark Twain

Argue for your limitations and, sure enough, they're yours. – Richard Bach

Low self-confidence isn't a life sentence. Self-confidence can be learned, practiced, and mastered – just like any other skill. Once you master it, everything in your life will change for the better. – Barrie Davenport

The way to develop self-confidence is to do the thing you fear and get a record of successful experiences behind you. – William Jennings Bryan

Don't wait until everything is just right. It will never be perfect. There will always be challenges, obstacles, and less than perfect conditions. So what. Get started now. With each step you take, you will grow stronger and stronger, more and more skilled, more and more self-confidence, and more and more successful. – Mark Victor Hansen

A few patterns emerge from the above quotes.

1. Confidence is a change that stems from both outward and inward appearances. It can begin with either one, and frankly I don't think I would prefer one over the other. If you start with external changes… you will look good which will make you feel good. That mood and confidence will eventually permeate through the rest of your life. After all, if you can revamp your physical appearance to be objectively attractive, there's no telling what you can't do!

2. A large component of confidence is the stock we put into how other people perceive us. This may not be ideal, but it's where it starts. Thus, we can take a lesson from this in observing other people's actions and assigning confidence values to them. Be extremely analytical and apply those changes and suggestions to yourself.

3. On some level, any confidence you show will be irrational. It's just the nature of the beast. Even Michael Jordan, who has all the reason in the world to be confident, can sometimes be overly so and irrational. But that doesn't mean he doesn't have a wealth of things to offer. You also do. Don't let the fear of appearing arrogant or immodest turn you off of projecting confidence, because it *will* happen. Get over that mental hurdle, and move on.

4. Once you believe you don't have confidence, you won't. Confidence starts with a belief in yourself, no matter how small. Pick one thing that you're great at – possibly the best at in the world. Take pride in it, and realize you are also allowed to have those feelings of pride in things that you aren't the best at. Maybe you aren't even good at them.

5. Failure breeds confidence. Why? Because when you have failed, you know how badly things can go... and yet the world didn't end. Failures eventually turn into successes, which also breeds confidence. It's the process that is important.

6. Conditions will never be ideal for you to build confidence. It all has to start somehow and somewhere. But it's within you.

7. Everyone has insecurities. But true confidence is security in who you are. Your insecurities are likely insignificant to many other people's... and ti is rare that they would never come up because everyone is so focused and self-conscious about their own. Your insecurities also add to your character because they haven't killed you yet. In that way, they actually signal that you are strong and still here.

Confidence can take you to your highest heights if you allow it, and it's something that you cannot compromise about yourself. Here are some actionable traits of a confident Jerk Complex to get you started on your journey.

1. Lead others and don't be a follower
2. Don't care if others don't follow
3. Don't seek approval or affirmation from others
4. Don't be a people pleaser
5. Invest in and value yourself
6. Accept and let in the fear – it's natural

True confidence is so because of its disregard not for others, but for what others think. It's a powerful trait that is magnetic, attractive, and increasingly rare.

14. Be a source of inspiration and challenge.

Enter the remora fish.

The remora fish is essentially a giant mouth with a fish body attached to it. It attaches itself to the underbelly of any sizeable shark and can remain there for its lifetime just feeding off the nutrients that the shark provides. It is a wholly unbalanced relationship in which one party is completely exploited at the expense of the other. Does this sound familiar?

Enter *Flowers for Algernon*.

Flowers for Algernon is a short novel by Daniel Keyes about a mentally retarded man who receives a surgery that turns him into a genius. He becomes incredibly self-aware, yearns for more in his life, and generally has his life enriched by the surgery. (For the purposes of this chapter, we'll ignore the part where the surgery's effects are only temporary, and he reverts back to his original mental state...)

In your relationship, are you a remora fish that only takes and doesn't give, or are you the mental retardation surgery that enriches someone's life? Moreover, is the woman the remora fish or the surgery to you?

The goal for a truly healthy relationship, and one that can make marriage a not-so-scary proposition is to encourage mutual self-growth and development. Ideally, a couple grows and develops together, and continues to find new ways to enrich their lives. This is simply not possible if either party is a remora fish.

In fact, guess what being a remora fish leads to?

You will be taken for granted.

You will become an afterthought.

You will become resented.

Worst of all, she will lost her respect for you because you wouldn't be bringing anything to the table. If you don't challenge, motivate, or inspire her, you will essentially become a body pillow. You'll have a physical presence and you'll be around to talk to her, but at best you will turn into a mere presence like a lamp.

Let's think for a moment about how the True Jerk challenges a woman that he is dating. He probably isn't doing it on purpose. He challenges her sense of attraction by not being available or entirely interested in her. He challenges her sense of self and identity by not truly taking an interest in her and making her self-conscious and question herself. Finally, he challenges her by being not entirely nice to her, so she is forced into defensive and argumentative modes around him.

The True Jerk doesn't challenge and inspire so much as prod and provoke. The short term effects might be similar, but the long term effects are stunningly different.

The Jerk Complex realizes that relationships are about bringing out the best in each other, and that it takes effort and focus to do so. A relationship should be a vehicle for becoming better people – one that simultaneously supports, challenges, and inspires.

So how do you add value in such a powerful way and avoid becoming a remora fish?

It starts with yourself. The Jerk Complex has his own expectations for himself, and it's a combination of seeing those expectations and choice encouragement that will challenge and inspire your woman. When you are a challenge yourself, you become a challenge.

The Jerk Complex empowers his woman by cheering for her, supporting her, and asking tough questions that will help boost her to the next level whether personally or professionally. He doesn't just go through the motions when talking with her.

He is a high value person, which can encourage his woman to become so as well in every aspect. He takes his own professional and personal risks. He is ambitious. He works hard to cultivate a healthy relationship, and calls her out if she is not putting forth the same effort. He has little fear of failure and doesn't forego pursuing what he wants in life. He has a thirst for adventure and life in general, and doesn't accept being a couch potato with Netflix every night.

He is spontaneous and bold in his sex life and allows the woman to explore her own sexuality. He doesn't avoid confrontation just for the sake of it – he realizes that the greatest growth can often come from the catharsis of challenge and resolution.

Finally, and perhaps most importantly, he truly adds value to her life in a tangible manner by leading the relationship and teaching her new things.

It all comes down to what you envision your happy relationship looking like. The best kind is a balance of minds that contributes to mutual growth and development. Once you ensure that you yourself are challenging and inspiring, you can and should impart the rest to your partner.

15. Vulnerability is your goal.

Women simply eat up the fact that I was a near-obese infant and adolescent. Why?

Just as I had a confidence chapter earlier, this is the vulnerability chapter – arguably, the most supreme and evolved form of confidence. If confidence itself is a game-changer, consider vulnerability re-writing the rules of the game itself.

If it's not clear yet, I'm a big fan of embracing vulnerability as part of your identity and how it carries over into your relationships.

Vulnerability isn't a sob story or being a sensitive push over. When I refer to vulnerability, I mean expressing yourself without shame or apology, embracing opposition and rejection by others, and willing to take risks for your beliefs and values.

It's the principle of recognizing who you are and what you stand for, and being amazingly comfortable with it. When you're comfortable with yourself, others become comfortable with you too, and it has a certain way of putting people at ease.

Vulnerability draws others to you, and instantly makes you attractive in the sense that you are so comfortable with yourself that you can express yourself without caring about the reaction from others. It shows a sense of proactivity and introspection, as you have principles and stances based on your beliefs.

Most of all, vulnerability allows you to display supreme confidence in yourself, whether you really feel that way or not. Putting yourself out there is an admirable act, and most people will be in awe and envious of you instead of putting any judgment on you like you might think.
And that might be the root of why the jerk, true or not, is attractive. They project the air that they are content with who they are, and don't mind if you object at all. While the outwards appearance is the same, the internal intentions and principles that govern them are extremely different.

The True Jerk, as I've discussed before, accomplishes the veneer of vulnerability by hugely overcompensating and overstating his abilities on many things before admitting to miniscule chinks in his armor. His ego can't survive a direct hit and unveiling of his true vulnerabilities, so he masks them with the appearance of not caring, and takes things personally later.

This leads to him attacking and lashing out at others when they open up and show their vulnerabilities because they sense an opportunity to make themselves seem more confident... at the expense of others.

I'm sure we can all name about 5 people off the top of our heads that partake in this.

When the Jerk Complex truly allows vulnerability and puts a certain amount of judging power into the hands of other people, it's a powerful gesture. He doesn't have to step on anyone to maintain his confidence, and can even find the humor in his flaws and judgments that other people impose on him. People, not just women, tend to gravitate towards those that are straightforward and aren't attempting to be something they are not. They'll know what they are getting, and will in turn open up to you in a way that you ever thought possible.

So back to my opening statement for this chapter – why do women love the fact that I was a Michelin baby and adolescent?

It's a fact that I find hilarious about myself. Many people can often relate to it. It disarms people and shows that I don't take myself that seriously. It shows that I have no issues letting chinks like that slide, and that I don't care if they tend to diminish my overall image. Most of all, I'm confident enough in myself to turn something potentially embarrassing into a uniquely vulnerable connecting point.

I am who I am, and you can accept me or not. And more often than not, after I share it, I get back something that they are insecure or that makes them vulnerable, and an instant deep bond is created.

Let's look at the other side:

If I was to be ashamed of this small fact, how would it reflect on the rest of my self-image and how others could deal with it? They would know that it's a sore spot, and would have to avoid it altogether. Tensions rise, and must be diverted.

A Jerk Complex's ability to be the attractive man that a woman desires in a relationship is directly proportional to how vulnerable he is willing to make himself. Vulnerability is what communicates a man's desires, and if they are actually expressed. Given the running theme that women want a take-charge, masculine mate, this is significant.

The flip side, of course, is the passive male who can only claim ownership to the pants of a relationship once in a blue moon. He doesn't freely express his opinion, quite possibly is a pushover, and seeks to please people (in this case, the woman of the relationship) instead of live his own life.

The passive male is mired in his passive label because he doesn't make himself vulnerable – he's simply not willing to take the leap of attempting to assert himself or open himself up to judgment in any way.

Vulnerability is an often overlooked element of attraction and self-esteem. Of course, even though I've told you how people subconsciously embrace the presence of vulnerability and impart a slew of positive adjectives to it, it doesn't mean that you won't have your mental blocks preventing you from immediately telling people your business.

Vulnerability is a process, but is one well-worthy of conquering as the pinnacle of confidence.

Conclusion

Now who can tell me the difference between a True Jerk and the Jerk Complex?

I'm looking for something to the effect of... the True Jerk manifests attractive features and traits because he simply doesn't care about the women he sees. Distance, apathy, and a lack of prioritization are, strangely enough, what women are attracted to. On the flip side, the Jerk Complex actually cares about the women he sees, but has learned to cultivate attraction by harnessing the True Jerk's traits to holistically improve his habits and lifestyle.

Here's the final translation for this book: the True Jerk is attractive because he puts up a front, while the Jerk Complex is attractive because he doesn't have to front.

I hope you realize the powerful lesson herein that you can remain your true self – the nice guy, the caring guy, the guy who will always be there – and yet attract women with the best and baddest jerks out there. If you follow my tenets within, you'll have truly impacted your entire life and upgraded yourself in every way imaginable.

The Jerk Complex is a mindset and a lifestyle that, just by gaining awareness of it, can skyrocket you into the stratosphere and help you conquer goals you never thought possible.

Women *want* to love guys like you, and you now have the tools to step up and announce your presence to them.

Finish last? This nice guy never will again.

Sincerely,

Patrick King

P.S. If you enjoyed this book, I would really appreciate if you left me a review on Amazon!

Some of my other works include:

Charm Her Socks Off: Creating Chemistry from Thin Air: http://www.amazon.com/dp/B00IEO688W

CHATTER: Small Talk, Charisma, and How to Talk to Anyone: http://www.amazon.com/dp/B00J5HH2Y6

Did She Reply Yet? The Gentleman's Guide to Owning Online Dating (OkCupid & Match Edition): http://www.amazon.com/dp/B00HESY42G

The Jerk Complex cheat sheet.

1. Chase her and she'll run away.

If you chase too much, too openly, too obviously, or too strongly, your pursuit will make her run from you like a gazelle. There's nothing attractive about being pursued so single-mindedly, and will lead to her devaluing you.

2. If you create a vacuum, she will fill it.

When you pull away, you create a vacuum that she will immediately want to fill… a process that turns her into the pursuer and can change the perception of the relationship's dynamics completely.

3. Dependence is the ultimate buzzkill… and is so having total control.

Maintain your independence from a woman, because if you start becoming dependent on her, you've robbed her of her own independence and given her total control… both of which are justified grounds for getting bored and losing respect for you.

4. <u>You are you, and she is only part of that.</u>

Your partner wants an equal and someone they can go toe-to-toe with. Prioritize your own interests and hobbies and don't make decisions based simply on wanting to spend time with her. You are not defined by her or the relationship.

5. <u>Anticipation is a super magnet.</u>

Anticipation and the lack of certainty is an incredible aphrodisiac and will draw women to you. Prolong the "chase" by simply being a busy person, and not artificially manipulating your availability.

6. <u>Act the prize, be the prize.</u>

When you perceive yourself as a high-value person, you act like it, and everyone else will follow your lead. Don't accept when others treat you like a backup or otherwise, because that will snowball.

7. <u>Treat her like a woman, not a daughter.</u>

A father nags, dotes, and is a general nuisance that makes his daughter want space and separation. A mate takes care of his woman and ensures her safety, but does so in a way that is more primal, subtle, and only creates more attraction.

8. <u>Space is power.</u>

When you give a woman space, who knows what she'll do with it. However, when you take the same space that she might want from you, and she notices, she will likely regret her choice immediately and want to close that space.

9. You Tarzan, she Jane.

Sexism be damned, women want a man who will take control, can dominate a relationship at times, and generally wears the pants. Do these things not out of chivalry, but because you are a dominant type of man, and it will pay dividends.

10. Embrace relationship limbo.

Resist the urge to define and spell out your feelings on where you want or see your relationship going until it is absolutely necessary. Again, uncertainty builds sexual tension, desire, and wanting.

11. You do not negotiate with terrorists (relationships).

Prioritize yourself and don't negotiate your own values or interests for the good of a relationship. Maintain a strong sense of self because when you are engaged, you become engaging.

12. No man taken for granted.

Do not act in a way that enables others to take you for granted, and react appropriately when they do. Don't be afraid to make waves or assert yourself.

13. The confidence chapter.

True confidence stems from being comfortable with your flaws and the realization that no one cares about them because they are too consumed with their own.

14. Be a source of inspiration and challenge.

Don't be a remora fish. Add value to her life by ensuring that you are challenging and inspiring yourself – and she will follow suit.

15. Vulnerability is your goal.

When you're comfortable with your vulnerabilities and flaws, it puts others at ease and makes them open up to you in ways you never thought possible. Vulnerability is also the height of real confidence.

Made in the USA
Lexington, KY
03 March 2015